THE DOG'S HEART

ALSO BY ELAINE TERRANOVA

.

POETRY

THE CULT OF THE RIGHT HAND

DAMAGES

TRANSLATION

IPHIGENIA AT AULIS

THE DOG'S HEART

ELAINE TERRANOVA

ORCHISES

WASHINGTON

2002

Library of Congress Cataloging-in-Publication Data

Terranova, Elaine.
The dog's heart / Elaine Terranova.
p. cm.
ISBN 0-914061-90-0
I. Title.
PS3570.E6774 D64 2002
811'.54—dc21

2001021361

ACKNOWLEDGMENTS

"Blind Man"	*Boulevard*
"The Cleansing"	*Bridges*
"Diabole"	*Parnassus*
"Floater"	*The Cortland Review*
"Letter Home from Santa Monica"	*Poet Lore*
"Merry-Go Round"	*Boulevard*
"Ministry to the Jews"	*Bridges*
"Necessity"	*The Virginia Quarterly Review*
"Night Blooming Cereus"	*Antioch Review*
"The Ruin"	*Pleiades*
"Sarajevo"	*The Christian Science Monitor*
"Saving the Art Teacher"	*River Styx*
"Secret Meanings"	*Boulevard*
"Skirt"	*Prairie Schooner*
"The Spot"	*The Virginia Quarterly Review*
"Thief"	*River Styx*
"White Leather Tango Gloves"	*Crab Orchard Review*

"The Stand-Up Shtetl" won the Anna Davidson Rosenberg Award in 1992.

Grateful acknowledgment is made to the NEA for a fellowship during which time this manuscript was completed.

Cover painting courtesy of The More Gallery

Manufactured in the United States of America

Orchises Press
P. O. Box 20602
Alexandria
Virginia
22320-1602

G 6 E 4 C 2 A

To My Brother Leo

TABLE OF CONTENTS

I

II

III

IV

I

I push away a nearly
irresistible sleep
to follow her in her pale gown.

Our flashlights braid
wide swathes of green on the lawn.

"We plant it," he'd said,
"then wait for it to surprise us."
She had outwaited him.

Then one day, a tiny pearl appeared
in the notch of a leaf. And now,
oh, most astonishing,
the universe poised
between expansion and collapse,
above a half-moon, rocking,
we stumble into its scent,
which, like memory itself, seems
to release heat, to increase disorder.

Light separates the petals.
We watch the oily, white socket dilate
as something stabs out
like an infant's fist, and is held,
throbbing, in the present.

BLIND MAN

He will not see those first golden notches
that open the tree to light.
But maybe for him the day
is just an emptiness, a great relief.

So much never reaches his eyes.
They don't curve toward the sight.
Say it is a ball rolling toward him
or some faraway, godawful accident.
He stands unaffected,
perhaps only reaching his hands deeper
into the pockets of confusion.

Zigzagging that white stick,
he is like the great sea turtle
in its box of water, flipping aside
what it cannot use.
And if the blind man is hungry,
sooner or later an apple
will rattle his plate.

Yet how much easier it is to tell a story
where the details shine.

Think what the dog would see
that the man doesn't see, what the cane would,
without an elbow of help. Think of
rooms that contain the threat even
of one other person, rooms that stop themselves.
And what of the tricks that are played
on the blind man, all the tricks
that are played in the dark?

Suppose he must get out of the house
and opens the door to a first step,

so wide in the imagination.
To wind and the leaves jangling,
turning their backs to their shadows,
those trembling eclipses of light.

FERAL GIRL FOUND IN A SUBURBAN HOUSE

We know her by the two perfect
sets of teeth, that grew in
like a shark's, one within the other.
Or when we speak, the way she stares
at a spot just over our shoulders
that seems more forgiving.

She is small and bent, as if
prepared to spring. She'd been strapped
for hours to the potty chair,
a creature like herself, hugging
the ground. The gods she invented
must have squatted on their haunches.

She doesn't feel heat. Her skin
is moist and cool like something
taken from a wood. Locked in her closet,
she played with two plastic raincoats,
red and green, and learned
to move sidewise like a beam of light.
She came out spitting and scratching.

Out of the noise surrounding her,
birds, lawn mowers, thunder,
she pulled the syllables
for food, one long vowel. For no,
a hiss that gives nothing away.

It is daylight still
but I have gotten inside, who knows,
the way the worm
gets into the dog's heart.
These houses,
I tell you, are heartless.
They seem all light and air,
that glass, a skin
as fragile as an animal's.

But upstairs
a man may be lying on his back
until a gulp or start wakes him.
How long I stand listening
for that tread I fear
from the floor above.

I've stepped into
a room all reds and greens,
the soft, sharp points of Persian rugs,
of mohair furniture
I rub myself against.
I hold a bone china box
up to the light and a lovely,
calm emptiness
opens before me.

I walk through a doorway without doors
then another, taking up
knick-knacks pining for use
and breathe on them.
No one for years has been so kind.

From here I look out and see
the last of the sun bond
to the gingko leaves, that gilding

so like astonishment.
Then a wind stirs the branches.
I am aware of this circling
from the ground up.
Inside me too there's something
that can't stop.

Even now a woman
may be leading an aproned boy
back with her groceries.
I feel that swivel of my neck
to the outside door, to the place
where the action happens.
Oh, what do I steal
but a little of her happiness?

I could test each wall
for another way out.
But the dog is in the yard,
big Doberman with his awaiting bark.
Also, the roll of a high, dark hedge.
Surely, though, I am safe. Surely
I can open the refrigerator yet
and in a cloud of light
drink deeply the milk
of whoever lives here.

BREAKING COVER

I

I grew up in the church. I learned
it was holy to serve. I had faith in love
and the power of blood to heal.
Then how could I have behaved otherwise?

It began with a news shot on TV. Far away,
a smiling man lay in an unpaved street.
You might have thought that this
was happiness but for the fly
crawling along the shining teeth. It began

with civil war. Not Viet Nam: our own.
Our fathers asked us to pay with our blood
for their mistakes. When we said no,
they sent their armies to our campuses.

A woman under sentence half my life,
I shut it out with tiredness
like a guillotine in the dark.
The old fallings off, the old quarrel no one
any longer has a use for. Listen,

when I was a child we got a dog
from the pound. If you picked up her paw,
she'd moan piteously. Or if
you took out a broom to sweep. So we knew
she must once have been abused.
Any pain like that shakes down
inside you and comes to light
like dust in sunlight. That's memory.

17

II

For days after the crime,
in a cramped, dirty room, I'd watch
the silent scattering of roaches
or read stained news from backstairs bins
by one dim light. I'd read a while,
then sometimes dig my hands
into my body, as if to lift it
out of this mire where it sank.

Soon, I hitched past fields
and herds of cows drawn up against the rain.
It fell so heavily, a sound
like a crowd closing around you.
I went as far as if I were Odysseus,
and someone still might recognize
the oar I carried on my shoulder.

III

Someday, they say, the earth
will begin to move
in 50-day orbits around the sun. Still,
something would manage to live in that cold.

With each new town I took a name.
My life was this impersonal,
people in the same place seeming
so much alike, who share the same mountain
or ocean, the same view
of the world. Now I've left them wondering

how a person who is kind
in unexpected ways might also be thoughtless,
or even have a thought toward evil.

If only we could know each other
by scent, as surely as an animal.

IV

I'd think from year to year,
"The picture they post
will look like you for a while,
then they will find another. And when they come
it will be like hunters flushing grouse."
Noisy, outraged birds. Startled,
they rise up and flap wings wildly
against any low branch, harming
only themselves. I wanted the harm behind me.

All this time, Viet Nam went on.
What we did, didn't stop it.

Again and again, I'd start up like a weed
out of an earth rich with the dead.
Their many dead, our one.

And if I say I only drove the car—
knew nothing of a silent alarm,
had not heard the shots— Until
the TV afterward spread among us
the officer's death on its beam of light.

V

This year, the year I've come back
to stand trial, the whole midsection
of the nation's under water.
Fields, silos, stands of trees.
And still the rains came on, my plane
skimming the flood like a great bird

with an olive branch in its beak.
I looked down at the badges of farms.
A new channel of the Missouri that met
the swollen Mississippi. Running away
is also termed flight. I turned back
to find again the family I left, the self.
Wave after wave, the sadness left me.
I had returned to the country of the living.

VI

At my parents', I look out at the sun
as it passes through the beaded curtain
of rain. A moth is trapped
between the window and the screen.
I think to myself, "It would have to be
Houdini to get out of there alive."
Outside, the leaves so bright,
their yellow trembling lights the room.
The wind builds like a cheer
through the grasses. When I entered again
that house I know better
than any other, I cried to see
how they had kept my small spinet piano
all these years, draped with a cloth
like a coffin bearing a flag.

The lights of earth come out like stars.
On the hillside, cows hunch like tombstones.
Each makes a plea in the dark.

Out of a tunnel, the yellow beams of cars.
Perhaps I am dead. Perhaps I am being shown
the lights of earth. They come out like stars.

Houses winking shyly, spark by spark,
the wild red hair of asparagus overgrown,
each makes a plea in the dark.

The bright face of the past is never far.
We move, half-blind, in a realm of time alone.
Then the lights of earth come out like stars.

Orange lamps swing out on poles in the park
into the unexpected, the unknown.
Each makes its plea in the dark.

Across the patent leather of the lake, winds moan,
and who is not aware within us of shining bone?
The lights of earth come out like stars.
Each makes a plea in the dark.

We drive on, hoping for fair weather,
but it's gray Connemara. There is only rain,
or mist that is an afterthought of rain.
And by now it's night, which muddies everything.
Without meaning to, we've passed the town,
rain swirling past in the gutters. We're lost
without human markers, until I spot on our map
the shrine and two bisecting roads. The sign

says B & B, and we take the clear path of light
into someone's parlor. She's lively, ginger-haired.
She sets out tea for us, settles us beside
a sweet turf fire. She tells us where we are—
so near the North a TV crew is shooting
a documentary on The Troubles.
"Anyhow, we've our own troubles here."
As if the curse of a powerful enemy
were enough to rot the bones.
For by then, I've spotted him, his face
gray as a pot. Even seated, he's a giant.
She says, "He used to be a bouncer."
A tiny, red-haired girl is flickering
at the doorway. "So ill. Must tell the kids.
They know he isn't right." And I see what he,
what we are all depending on,
her continuing voice and the hearth
with its steady thread of flame.

"There are no windows
at the shelter." How can
she see daylight? And,
"You don't eat unless you work."

She must flush the halls
end to end with water,
snap hospital corners on the beds.
At night a flashlight
pins her to the mattress.
What she carries in and out,
all that she's collected
from her life, gets broken
into smaller and smaller pieces
like the bones of a saint.

No wonder she will slip away.
Not some showy place,
not a corner with her hand out.
But back into doorways, under bridges.
When she gets a dollar,
eat what she wants. Happy to sleep
with the winding sirens.

Then, hour by hour,
the sun drops down
a little closer, the birds swing
from branch to branch
like great chords of music.

THE RUIN

1

Is the ruin a shell or a skeleton?

We passed the smoking banners
of the nuclear plant going into its country.
Nuns and pilgrims, soldiers also
have been travelers here.

2

In the photo the ruin
seems all there is. Really, though,
a rope and empty space
are needed to set it apart. It is as if
they'd wanted to scratch this one place
clear of all connection. Otherwise
it would be just the past continuing.

3

The ruin's rectangles and perfect circles
seem a sequence of development and decline.

Don't you remember the road here?
At first, like anywhere,
a white church, a river curling.
Then quarry, dam, mill, every stop

a power point, which is clear in the names
our fathers gave them, something
they meant to tell us.

4

Perhaps the ruin is a tool to measure
the transit of heavenly bodies,
for we know that its main axis
aligns with the sun on the longest day.

Therefore, the sky is the real structure here.
The ruin is only broken teeth in its mouth.
Long ago, the sun rose

in the niche between rocks, as it does now.
If it rose to the left, there would be
a rainy season, to the right,
a season for hunting and war.

5

The ruin parts the grass
as the grass once broke through stone
for the long time when people
forgot how to live in cities.

6

We must pay an admission fee.
At sunset red flares rise in a spray
again from the ruin's depths. Should we applaud?

SARAJEVO

Play on,
Vedran Smailovic,
cellist for the opera.
Others have stopped practicing.
They say, "For What? We live like rats,"

while for these 22 days
you put on formal dress
and sit outside the bakery
to play Albinoni's *Adagio*,
that series of beginnings
which rises and rises
out of itself.

The music's dark wings
must close over you
to keep you safe,
as shells pierce
the surrounding air,
fire answering fire.

You play once
for each
of the 22 hungry citizens
killed by mortar blast
as they stood here in line for bread.

THE STAND-UP SHTETL

Not until a shtetl had its own cemetery was it truly considered a Kehillah Kedosha, a
Holy Community in Israel.
—*The Paper Shtetl: A Complete Model of an Eastern European Jewish Town*

Let the wind and rain start with a sigh,
over and over. Then you who have forgotten,
you who never knew, cut out the paper pieces;
score and fold them back. Where the instructions
call for bending or curling, determine
how far to bend, how tightly to curl.

It is nearly *Rosh Hashonah*. The blacksmith
is forging good luck for all this new year.
Likewise, the feather plucker, with his goose down,
is laying the groundwork for a year's
innocent sleep. "From your mouth to God's ear,"
the townspeople greet one another,
although some will wander, with open collars,
with exposed throats, into the path
of thundering Cossacks. You may ask, Is this
where it leads, all the whispering to God?

Still, it is remarkable, how these characters
can be cut out of the bitter story
whole and looking so well.
Those two young girls trading secrets
by a tree, who stare into each other's faces,
are a single piece made with one V fold.

The nearest house is in darkness.
But when the walls of the next are folded back,
they form right angles with a newly swept floor.
Push out the chimney with a pencil and smoke curls.
The woman inside lets the boiling water
hurry her. The Sabbath feast is approaching.
Bend the woman's head forward. Fold her arms
over her eyes, carrying the darkness to them

27

as she makes her blessing over the candles.
Now the shames, who all week ferries
the smaller boys to chedar, knocks
on her shutter, bringing the Sabbath.

Horses, goats and chickens feed in the yards.
Each has a right and a left side,
touching back to back, though only one tail.
Curve the horse's neck gently, likewise,
the goat's. Bend the tail down and the legs in,
slightly, for balance and to make them stand.

Move on to the market. Take up this man,
the peddlar. Perhaps he is a buyer
of the clothes of the dead. Bend him
forward at the elbows, allowing him to grip
his pushcart. As you do, watch him look up
from under that forward-jutting cap
which focuses his will and concentration.
Bend one leg forward and the other back.
His is a sad business. Expect him
to appear exhausted by it or discouraged.

Then turn a corner to the synagogue.
It is formed of two connecting pieces.
No cuts or marks should be made
on the unseen, inner side. Curl the rabbi's beard
and tilt it behind the podium. Put a bend
in the Torah reader's back. He should look down
at the words, not insolently up into God's eye.

Leave space at the center for a wedding.
As the bride and groom grind the wineglass
of misfortune underfoot, bend the musician's right arm
around in front until his bow strikes the violin.
Then arrange the men in a semicircle, dancing.
Lift their knees. Fling their arms around
each other's shoulders, so that, kicking and bouncing,

they are open to anything.
Each step in their dance will move the world forward.

Do not forget the dead we keep with us always.
On the right, fold the headstones upright,
those for the chairmaker and the tailor, and for
the water carrier whose father and grandfather

were also water carriers. Group the graves
to form a cemetery. The state may forbid this,
since the dead lay claim to the earth.
But if a cemetery is allowed, stand the trees
on the angle formed at the base. Bring in
a watchman and paid mourners. Bow the trees down
in the wind or extend them like the wings
of enormous birds. Bend the darkest branches
outward to surround it, to cherish it.

II

THE CURRENT

Two swans, affixed
to the mirror of the river,
to each other. Until one,
in widening circles,
copies the loose cast
of the hawk above. He rocks
and dips. A separation
of feathers. One wing
acts as a rudder.

He goes only as far
as an emerging shoal, but she
comes effortlessly forth
to meet him. What moves her
is what moves the water:
the current. What is happening
right now. The drift. The wind.
The pull of him.

Bougainvillea floats on the surface
of the hotel pool, is banked when I wake
like pink fluorescent snow

against my door. This afternoon
I walked along the ocean, my shadow
stretching out before me. The sun warmed

only one side of my face. Here
it is always beautiful. Santa Monica,
"Home of the Homeless," the radio says.

And I pass the many homeless in the shoreside park,
all they own, rolled up underneath them.
Soup kitchens are set up on the beaches.

Last night at a party a woman asked
if I were married. I almost had to think.
She'd never lived with anyone, never shared

the same physical space, gliding past one another
as if under water. "I would be lost," she said,
her lover close enough to hear.

"I need to get up early. He can't stay."
And I see this adds a poignancy.
She thinks of love as an abduction,

a robbery. Right now, I'm listening
to that Brazilian jazz I love, just loud enough
to know that the words aren't English

but a soft cajoling. The point is,
I am not meant to understand, the words,
a flowering I put before me in my nakedness,

as if it were your name. Maybe that woman
is right not to spend all night with him,
the secret part, where she'd surprise him.

But I think that night itself
leaves us helpless. Things break down then,
and what if there is no one to fix them?

The ferns uncoiling,
the fir trees shooting out
their first bright extensions,
you go off to clear a path
between living trees.
It is almost dusk.
I watch the sun slide off
the tips of leaves.
Then a wind is circling
bushes and weeds.
Even the trees start to move
in wide figure eights.
Maybe by now you've reached
the dump at the edge of the road,
that mountain of decay
smelling of crushed plaster and rust,
where dead sunflowers
duel with iron rods. I can hear
the chastening cry of the crows.
Then a tanager plummets like
a drop of blood.

FLOATER

I had to push myself
away from the window to watch TV,
even the Democratic convention,
police marching behind shields
like gladiators.

And all that summer, I was mindful
of what I was using up,
water, paper, daylight, the thoughts
going through my head.

Paula had lent me her apartment.
She'd gone to the country,
an abandoned farm where hunters wintered—
I imagined bats wheeling around
the dome of a barn, and below,
children on bikes, echoing their shrieks.
Later, parents who read bedtime stories
very fast, racing sleep.

I was here because I had walked out of my life.
I was a floater,
like those first-year birds
who wait for the chance to swoop down
and quickly replace the territorial bird.

There were plants to water,
but I could leave them, Paula said.
Dark green succulents
that stuck up like thumbs.
The tables were topped
with collections of shells and stones.

But so little could I find
in this place that I wanted,
string and fasteners in a kitchen drawer,

a melonballer. I ate
in the coffee shop around the corner
where cakes were left in a glass pillar,
their icings hardening like paint.

Once, I let in the immigrant janitor
to fix a leak, but after that
I kept it dark and no one came.

I pedaled air. I flew.
I cut a clean razor line
down the hill on his daughter's bike.
When the hay was bloody stubble,
I'd wait with her in the fields for deer
until the sunset drained
and her freckles faded. But no deer came.
Only an old screech owl, my familiar.
The child thought me a glittering creature.
The same quick joy lit our eyes
at a look from her father.
But it was her mother, after all,
under the covers. That woman
could hear the rain start to fall.
She herself gave me clothes
and a room at the top of the house.
The world's best muffins, as well,
and a recipe, yet some one ingredient
had been left out. That wild ride
I borrowed from the daughter.
I'd watch her plunge and struggle up,
zigzagging out of the way of snakes.
I took for a salute the bright flap
of her hair in the wind.
I'd have changed anything for her.
It was he, of course, who invited me.
I was sure there'd be nights out back in his arms,
when the rain came down like hoofbeats.
I grew like a tree in their midst.
I could tell that I choked them.
But, surely, his wife at least
might have heard, as my little white feet
hesitated at their doorsill,
the voices groaning behind me.

WHITE LEATHER TANGO GLOVES

I still pass that one lit square in the dark,
the apartment of those Latin Americans
where Pierre once brought me to a party,
a party, but where were the guests?

I put on the white leather gloves
I thought were a gift. They came up
over my elbow, hooking with small
covered buttons at the wrist. Shimmering,
elegant, they wrinkled like skin.
And I saw how a glove could be a token
of something else. How it bracketed a touch.

Uncle and nephew, they called themselves.
I came to believe, like us, they were lovers.
Still, they needed me. Men didn't dance with men.
I was the fuse of the music.

As Pierre sat silent in a corner, I danced
each dance. Tango after tango, arch and false.
It was a continuing melodrama,
yet something of the truth was moving in it.
The way he held me, the way he looked into my eyes,
for the young man this dance seemed a way out.

So many steps could have taken us very far
in any one direction, but then we'd turn
and start again. It was not a dance

so much as a series of wrong decisions.
Through the window, I saw how the moon
clung to the branches. And when the record stopped,
when the guitar or the accordion—whatever keyboard it was
someone had strapped across his heart—
stopped playing, I felt the breathlessness
you feel as you are shocked out of sleep.

Later, I'd think of those two men, busboy,
janitor, at what, in a grander city,
might have been the grand hotel. The gloves
were souvenirs, found in the nearly empty drawer
of a hotel room. A guest who had checked out

wouldn't go back, even to ask. The gloves
had covered the small red marks on my chapped hands
contacts with the world that show
I'm not careful. They took them back. Pierre,

as well, was sure they didn't fit. And when
would I have worn them again? Where music
wants you so much it is a direct address, or love
turns toward you and away at the same time.

A busy road bisects the cemetery,
makes a corridor through the dead.
Thin stones stagger on either side.
Descending, you can see to where

the shore is tacked on to ocean,
to where the harbor faces the sea
with beautiful, outstretched arms,
the suddenness of that blue edge.

Mimicking it, in the town and hidden,
is a horseshoe soda fountain,
where the toothless poor, like shipwrecks,
hunch over their coffees.

The whole town awaits
the cold touch of the rich. It is as if
they had buckled on sparkling shields
to come inland. Meanwhile, their yachts

shift from foot to foot
like jilted dancers. The widower who drinks
is hosing down his siding. His house
will bring a fortune in empty rooms.

Everyone has got an extra bed.
The plump housewife and the husband she keeps
give up their room to paying guests.

But in a garden where bloom toughens
to husk, a smell of death fills
a summer house. On windowsills, there's
the rustle of insects tumbled on their backs.
A sheet has been settled over a half-eaten meal.

There's just the two of them.
He's ill, she is assisting him.
They have begun to collect deaths,

the brother with Lyme disease, a father's stroke.
Clothes are piled into corners. "We're pack rats,"
she allows. Chairs sit on chairs.

From their porch you see a small
and beautiful island and an egret
guarding that island. The sun is almost gone,
though the sky in one small recess

is straining to be blue again.
On the pebble beach,
children nibble at jelly sandwiches
against an abandoned rowboat.

MOCKINGBIRD

Like the ceramic statuette
on the music box
my mother-in-law has
from her late husband,
calling to her
for some years until it went mute,

the mockingbird at school,
on its cyclone fence, lured
by red berries, sings as I pass,
without irony.

Today I spent an hour
helping a boy learn to write.
He smelled
of the disinfectant
clothes absorb in thrift stores.
I breathed it in. I kept that smell
alive in me a while.

The boy didn't mind school.
He minded going home to whatever
waited for him there. So we mouthed
the various sounds, the words
amassing like rock.

I could tell he was tired
of the circles I put
his hand through. The awkward strokes.
His thoughts kicking out against paper
as if this were swimming.

And I thought of Keats,
not much more than a boy. Inside
with his books and the heath

only steps away, the old trees
and ground so thick with acorns,
nothing grows underneath. Of how
I'd set my feet down on stair after stair
and lifted myself, going into his house,
as he must once have had the breath
to lift himself from that high iron bed.

The days I teach, I like to leave
while it's still sunny,
to go out to where the bird's voice
is rising. Watch him,
white wing patches coming to rest
from the wingbeats
slow enough to be counted.

Repeater of songs, perched now
with three toes in front, one long one
behind, singing, listening.

It wasn't meant to happen. Like a knife
that slips through bread
and into the first joint of your finger.
I was a woman in a dress and pearls.
My footing sure, the front of me
so carefully put together.

And this was a block of firmly closed doors.
Lawn after lawn, the green rectangles
going on forever. No razor wire
or stagnant gutters anywhere. No one ahead,
but one man moving toward me.

It was a summer afternoon. I'd been looking away,
studying the dead air beside me. We should
have passed like two bars of light,
but he grabbed my skirt and threw it
up over my shoulders.

Then, like a scene in a painting
that takes place half in the sky, I am where I am
and at the same time, locked out of my body.

I must have known this was nothing,
that worse went on within those walls.

That smear of sound, only a record started wrong,
something torn. For I stood there, hushed,
like a tree with fire at its heart.

Sometimes our houses shake in the night.
It may be thieves loosening the copper down spouts—

we are not far from boarded-up windows
you could beat and beat your fists against—

and sometimes, too, we hear sirens though
only a single laugh is left to glow in the dark.

Or that odd bird bleats its same, repeating signal
like a voice abstracted from a dialogue.

Not the bird whose song starts as flat statement,
then dips and flounders into melody. No.

That one would stop when the dark became impenetrable.
This bird goes on, a sound that is like white petals

fleeing from yard to yard. We can never find him,
though the moon, too, is an ardent hunter.

III

Here is the dark matter of memory:
the past, and how we retrieve it,
that reeling in of sentiment.

In my sleep I furnish the old house,
remembering first
one small mahogany side table.
Its middle shelf, crooked
like an elbow for books.

I go on filling up each room,
clearing my mind of the past,
as if to empty it.

Outside, block after block,
there is an evenness.
the white boxes of houses.
No charm. Rather, an arduous regularity.
Yet even here,
sometimes memory flares.

Fat child in the cold house.
Everything said to her, "Eat me.
It's good to keep you round like that."
And she made of her right hand's
four main fingers a fork.

At night, soft, muffled explosions
of car doors opening,
people shutting their houses behind them.

She couldn't sleep,
sleep was a stumbling block,
not the bell out in an ocean,
signaling shore.
In the burnt, back half of the house,
her parents tossing,
and over their palpitations, tics,
anywhere their bodies
might putt-putt, falter, stop,

she strains to hear,
on the red plastic radio
one brother bought her, a polka
moving out in all directions
like light from a star.

Behind the ivy and gauze curtain,
is a screen porch
where dark absorbs the light

of each known object.
All our days are tangled with shadow.

And where is the spiritual center
of such a place? Wherever
it is darkest. In the narrowest shoe
under the bed.

"He loves you. Look how he works
for you," our mother said. His work
was to grind down diamonds.
On dim afternoons in the little shop
the dust of what he did glittered
around him, until it fell in a greasy layer
at his feet. Sounds pierced
the crumbling white-washed walls.
He took these as the evil signals
of his neighbors. How cleverly
they monitored his thoughts,
sending their henchmen after him, coming
and going, while in his pockets,
the jewels nestled into the folds
of thin paper like good, brilliant children.
Coming home, he climbed out of the subway
into bright air, dragging his bad leg
behind him. Haste and rage boiled up in him.
Then he got to the door.

On the steep lawns
the neighbors favor rock gardens,
a few thin blooms, dearly won.

I see us as we come from school,
heads on chests, as if to say again,
"I'm sunk." And watch the infants
bundled in their mothers' care
being glided into dark interiors.

What comfort do we take
in these others, in ourselves?
When we're sent out to play,
hard stone steps
take us down to the street.

We line up on each side of the street.
We count to three and curse.

Baby curses, but still,
the single, same syllables
harden in our teeth. We ball
a fist around it, slick and sharp.
A stone is hate compressed.

And would we have thought
to thus strike out
but for her, that red-faced girl?
She brought a wildness from her
old neighborhood, standing alongside
her skinny brothers and sisters,
and with them a mild,
doe-eyed creature, my good friend.

And whoever was on my side
was crying out, "Go back
where you belong!"

They were survivors.
Where we lived there had been no war.
They felt safe in their own houses,
emptied of anyone else.
Even I knew this as safety,
maple tree I threw my arms around
when I skated home,
as if with love.

Though we all heard
the gusts through the halls
that came from nowhere,
that went nowhere.

my father called out,
when you moved in with your
unsmiling son, Mrs. Durstbrum,
contempt in his voice,
he couldn't keep it out.
For you had nothing,
less than us. Once here,
you didn't leave your house.
It sat attached, a dark mirror
of our own, so close
I might have entered it
through the back of a drawer

or a drainpipe. But an Atlantic
flowed between us. On your side
daylight was an accident,
a bad adjustment of the shades.
At four, I confused your name
with "dustbroom." You moved
as stiffly and had yellow hair.
What's more, you cleaned and cleaned.
And yet, in all our years
of living side by side, you did not
scatter or disperse a remnant of

your husband's awful death.
You were proud of your son,
with his scientific mind.
Maybe he saw, by the bright,
narrow light of mathematics,
some order to your experience.
Long after I had moved away,
I wondered when you'd vanished utterly.
Sweep, sweep, I should have said
to you sometime, Mrs. Dustbroom,
sweep Europe out of your heart.

Every day, my mother
pushed the wire grocery cart
before her like a cage.

That was when understanding
pierced my skin, a splinter
that would not come out,
though she pricked and pricked
my finger with her needles:

"Can't you be happy here with us?"

Ever after, each new place
has been only a spot
on the grid of my childhood.

Who, who was there now
to offer their intercession for her?
Father's one slap and the air
around her hot face shattered
in bewilderment. His one
caress when she fell
down the world's steps.
A trembling had come
over her body then, piano
never before, never again played.

"What will become of you,"
the professor later asked,
"double crossing your legs
as you do, at the knees
and again at the ankles?"
(Long, full legs.) That was
in English class, the clock,
ticking and slicing. She wondered
what his interest was.

Would she ever again
know intimacy, looking for years
into the same faces till they
were rubbed clear as glass?

IV

MERRY-GO-ROUND

Thus I become conscious
of the objects of the world,
little girl on a rusty
mechanical horse. Red buds
are sprouting on the trees
above my life. Days at school
I sit behind my desk, behind
a whole wooden consciousness,
waiting for the merry-go-round.

It is made from the parts
or ideas of animals. With a jerk,
they are hammering. So swift,
yet so still. That great, wheeling darkness
is the shadow of the canopy.
This is its barn, this is its stable.

Gilding and colored glass,
mirrors that flash back light.
Even plaster is important.
I see that the world
is not flesh, not straw. Not anything
that I find easily, loose
in the dirt. Oh, sculptured island,
no one has questioned your right

to turn, ever. Yet sometimes,
I would like my mind to let
the animals go, let them move off
through darkening trees
as the fireflies the riders
throw over their shoulders explode.

GETAWAY

What lives here
is unrepentant. Lizards.
Roaches that fly. Bushes
smelling of nothing—
someone has slashed
those red-veined shoots to a box.

And in the Florida room
boxes of photos weigh down
our laps. My aunt's thumb
rolls over the faces,
"He's dead. He's dead."
The past is a muscle
tightening in her throat.

Then, what is it
I reach out my hand to say?

Outside, people
walk home in couples, or paired
with their shadows.
They are going in circles,
70th Street, 70th Avenue,
70th Court. No one
can find a way out

among the dark
skeletons of palms.
Sometimes long-necked birds
set down on the lawns
their graceful, questioning bodies.
My aunt thinks they are dirty,
that they are all ducks.

Later, a moon of bone
knocks on the canal

that runs behind
the houses, reminder
of the marshes underneath,
and my aunt holds her breath
at the first orange spot
she finds in a linen cloth.

Now my unmet grandfather,
easygoing drunk,
is shaken down
from the family tree,

and dead Uncle Pete
with '30s bravado,
in argyle vest and knickers,
pointing a tommy gun.

He drove getaway for the Mob.
An elevator operator here,
from high windows
finding and losing
his bird's eye view of the sea.

Aunt, in New York
you dreamed this just reward.
A skylight over you
promising light, this backyard
where you gather oranges
you can reach,
beneath bright flights
you have no wish to name.

TIME TRANSFIXED

—after Magritte's painting

A train shoots through the fireplace.
In the mirror above it,
my father continues to straighten
his tie. He is dressed for winter,
woolen vest under the jacket of his suit.

Families on the train
sit in parallel lines, going back.
Outside, streets keep pace with the train,
though one can't see to the ends of them,
the sun not penetrating. A pair of lovers
lean close in their seats until quiet
falls between them like a curtain.

In our living room, my brothers and I
wear our resemblance as certain swans
wear their black masks. In all of us,
the soul moves in identical gestures,
what are known as *affetti*. Each night
at the same time darkness touches us.

A passenger is a beggar,
a homeless snail. That shared window,
that dull rectangle, like a painting
from the dime store, each invests
with his own significance.

After supper we are gathered together.
This happens every night. From where
we are, we come back, the false
in what we see and the bare walls
facing us. Until my brothers must cleave
to their wives, branching off,
as in the Bible, forearms shielding
their weeping eyes. But for the moment

I watch the firelight travel along
the hair of their arms like brushfire.

THE CLEANSING

When a knife meant for dairy
was used mistakenly to cut meat,
hadn't my mother, the same night,

plunged it into the ground*
to cleanse it, sure that the dirt
had power, that it forgave?

And what would they make of this,
those people who lived beside us?

Really, our houses were thrown
against one another, though
in my dreams there might be
a moon and a tree between us
or a silhouette of porch steps.

The boy once stood in his window,
taking off his pajamas
for me to see. The moonlight
fell over his front like quarters.

He'd beat me up as we walked
from school. No one could make him stop.
Our families no longer spoke.

This was hard, like
swallowing knives. We'd sit
on adjoining patios,
metal chairs whining, and look away.
We might have been set out in a desert.

Once I said so loud, I must have
meant them to hear, that what
was good about the A-bomb is,
we would all die at once.

*ritual connected to Orthodox Jewish dietary law

CAMP HOFNUNG

This is after those other camps,
the death camps,
and in a new country.

We children, these aged,
have come for our health,
for fresh air.

Nothing is green.
Ocher dirt. Ocher grasses.
Stick trees with the legs
of tall animals.
Sun, in the open, that stuns like a blow.

They have outlawed running.
Enough to go into the water,
to clothe yourself in God's nature.

But the water is too fast to swim in,
too shallow. They sprinkle it over them
as if it were holy
or rub it in like a salve.

Their veins are blue strings.
The deeply-creased faces
could break apart in your hands.
Yet I stare at them
as if I loved them.

Hofnung I know it means hope.
God's words, this Yiddish.
I've heard it at home in anger and grief.
It stings or it pricks you with guilt.

Then what do they make
of our childish babble

with their speech
that is black fire over white fire,
undivided into words?

MINISTRY TO THE JEWS

We were in a park. I'd left
my mother on a bench
beside her friend, the Christian
missionary.—Do I need to speak
of my mother's loneliness,
of her hunger for anyone's word?—

This was a stiff lady who smelled
of dead flowers. She had been
to China and Africa. I had from her
a small, crocheted cross
that I kept with my handkerchiefs.

I went off alone
to where the trees were thickest.
Leaves moved in the wind
like tinkling ornaments
and here and there embroidered tiny corpses
hung from spider webs.
On my finger was that ruby ring, my birthstone.

I watched a squirrel climb down head first
from the nearest tree, his eye
shining into my eye. Imagine!
He ate out of my hand.

Then, so quick I wasn't frightened,
he'd fastened his teeth
around the red stone and bit, hard.

A small, savage act.
Yet he didn't even break the skin,
leaving only these tiny marks in the gold
that have become part of the design.

SAVING THE ART TEACHER

As if you are a movie comic, an expert
in auto crashes, and the street slicked down
with water and soap, you stand
amid the hawks and squalls of cars.
All the figures on the street,

like the ones in your paintings,
carpenters, house painters, turned away
to live their own lives, the little boy on the corner
shimmering in sunlight, his body might be melting.

A few blocks away even the river,
that is sometimes green, sometimes a churning brown,
is white as a line of thin air.
You yourself are not looking, your step

launched to meet the traffic, only your shadow
lolling back toward me. Now my hand
reaches out to save you. As it does, the world flattens.
Isolated and enlarged, we are the key figures.

And I remember how you held your death with you,
secret, pocketed, crab hand, scuttling out of sight.
The other hand was a genius. Those Saturdays, you taught
that the ripe fruit lived within itself, filled out
its allotted space, the spread table cascading
toward the eye. All morning you came back
with your pencil, good hand prodding my wayward one,

that fidgeted at trees, at some bird not in the guide
but still to me a plausible bird, with its thin,
wistful tail. You came to see how the scratches developed,
how much time I wasted with my friends.

You cut through our high spirits like a cruel tooth.
But I listened, as I listened for

72

my parents' breath at night, assuring me
of my own continuing life. And I learned

a constant self-correction, yours the hidden hand
one lifts to curb the self. Yet was that all?
for I also learned to inflate the world with color,
which, for this long, has pleased me.

—for the painter Jack Bookbinder

THE SPOT

The spring my father died,
when I came to believe that everyone
was mortal, I found a spot at the back of my leg,
jagged and dark, that held on like a tick.
I waited for it to grow into a cancer.
First blemish, I thought, in a spoiling fruit.
So small, and yet a mark, a certainty.

I'd been in Egypt, studying the past.
One day, a colossus lay before me in sand
as if it had just fallen across my path.
A cart driver was taking me along the desert
to a buttery or a pottery, he might even
have been saying, leprosary. He couldn't
be stopped. We came at last to a Coptic church
where he showed me signs drawn
in old copy books, a blue-tiled emptiness.

I became aware of the spot as I climbed
up to my place in a vast arena.
I was looking down behind me at small,
scattering figures. The performance,
a circus or spectacle, just about to begin.

PORTRAIT OF MYSELF AND MYSELF

We sit for it
in white dimity dresses,
myself beside myself.
Below each throat
is the heart's red locket.

Several canvases
have been prepared
to record the effects
of mood or changing light.

The artist sees
that we are not identical,
sisters, perhaps, as pain
is a sister to desire.

He is a tree
that sways in the wind,
weighing one branch
against another.

Oh, I remember her as a child
testing all the vowel sounds,
finding a language
to carry the tune of thought.

Odd, how in one music
the instruments cry out
to each other, which is why
my childhood stung so.

Together, we rode
a carousel of fears. And when,
a stranger, you came to us hurt,
it was she who bandaged your wounds
with our longing.

NECESSITY

While I was young, while death
was still the exception,
turning up unexpected, shining,
like a coin at the bottom of my purse,
I lived for the first time
away from home, two floors up
from a furrier and just above
a Greek family
where a sister killed her brother.

Some Saturdays a deaf man
went from door to door selling needles.
And I'd thought, "Yes.
What a quiet activity it is,
to sew." I too lived
without the bewitchment of speech.
Even the sound of rain stunned me.
So I trembled to hear
the wretched mother keening.

Slowly, I filled up my small room—
the years at home had starved me
of myself. To say I was happy
is not exact. More,
like someone who agrees
to her own sacrifice or exile,
that it was necessary.

Night after night
the woman's wails rose up
through the floorboards.
I imagined her in black, rent clothes
with her double sorrow,
grief rising and falling back.
I imagined
that terrible rocking.

Each day as I passed beneath
the dark arch of the stairwell,
I waited for her
to wave away scarves and darkness
and emerge, clear-eyed, somehow reconciled.

DIABOLE

You know how night shuts down everything,
and it is only the moon that stands there,
beckoning?

Well, I am thinking of
Rembrandt's dark interiors, how he pulls
the person out of the shadows. "Woman with Pink,"
for instance. She is holding a flower before her
as if to light her way into the world.

Or of vampires, who can only live, if that
is what they do, at night—collectors
of loss, my friend, an expert, calls them,
dirt from the homeland, one or two

bartered Botticellis. Theirs is strictly
a literary existence, no roots, she'd say,
in the collective unconscious. That is why
they are beloved, creatures of longing,
as we are, for what has never been.

I did not go to the high school reunion.
Twenty known deaths so far.
Even our crewcut class president

who led cheers in white bucks,
raving against the dark. I hope my friend Ted
is still alive and no walking skeleton with AIDS.
Sometimes now, there's the same impatient rain
I remember from that time, with a brilliant sun
to follow, radiance behind everything,
like a view glimpsed in a rearview mirror.

Tonight, eating these half-withered, negative
little plums, the end of their season,
I am listening to Bach's *Partita* for solo violin.

Imagine the instrument,
pouring out its heart alone like that.